Crosswords for Kids

Trip Payne

Official
American Mensa
Puzzle Book

Sterling Publishing Co., Inc.
New York

Dedicated to my mother, Brenda Fleming, and my late father, Norman Payne, who both encouraged me to solve puzzles like these when I was a kid.

Edited by Peter Gordon

4 6 8 10 9 7 5

Published by Sterling Publishing Company, Inc.
387 Park Avenue South, New York, N.Y. 10016
© 1999 by Trip Payne
Distributed in Canada by Sterling Publishing
℅ Canadian Manda Group, One Atlantic Avenue, Suite 105
Toronto, Ontario, Canada M6K 3E7
Distributed in Great Britain and Europe by Chris Lloyd
463 Ashley Road, Parkstone, Poole, Dorset, BH14 0AX, England
Distributed in Australia by Capricorn Link (Australia) Pty Ltd.
P.O. Box 6651, Baulkham Hills, Business Centre, NSW 2153, Australia

Sterling ISBN 0-8069-1249-9

CONTENTS

INTRODUCTION

If you've never tried solving a crossword puzzle before, it's just like playing a video game, except that it's a lot less noisy, and there's not as much action ... and there's no joystick either. Well, okay, maybe it's not like a video game at all. Forget I said that.

The puzzles in this book are filled with things that you probably know a lot about—games, food, school, sports, music, and so on. There might be a word now and then that you don't know. Just remember, it's not "cheating" to ask someone else for help when you get stuck. In fact, it's a good way to learn something new. (And some of these words come up more than once, so after you learn them the first time, you can guess them by yourself the next time!)

I hope you enjoy this book of video games ... I mean, this book of crossword puzzles!

—Trip Payne

PUZZLES

1

ACROSS

1 How a baby might say "father"
5 "That's ___ bad!"
8 Item of clothing worn in winter
12 More than some: 2 words
13 Bone found in the chest
14 In addition
15 Chicago Bulls star of the 1990s: 2 words
18 Where your pupil and iris are
19 Have breakfast or lunch
20 Bruce ___ (Batman's secret identity)
23 Perform in a movie
24 You see stacks of it on farms
27 Gets older
28 Struck a match
29 "In ___ of emergency, break glass"
30 What old bananas start to do
31 Neither this ___ that
32 Place in the desert that's not so bad
33 You boil soup in this
34 Answer to an addition problem
35 Chicago Bulls star of the 90s: 2 words

42 "Mary ___ Little Lamb": 2 words
43 What the O stands for in "I.O.U."
44 Encourage
45 Finishes
46 ___ Flanders (Homer's neighbor on "The Simpsons")
47 Black gunk in a chimney

DOWN

1 A beaver builds it
2 Muhammad ___ (famous boxer)
3 One of the Seven Dwarfs
4 The capital of Greece
5 Many people decorate one for Christmas
6 It's used to stop a squeaking sound
7 Another word for "thing"
8 You push one in a grocery store
9 Like great-grandparents
10 Cool ___ cucumber: 2 words
11 2000 pounds
16 How a soldier says the word at 26-Down
17 One kind of grain

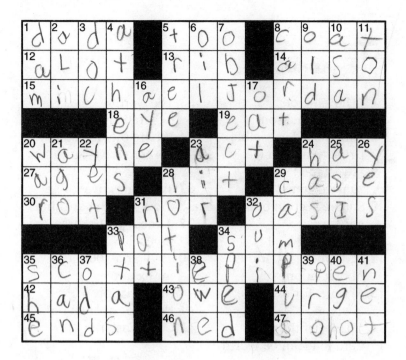

20 Card game that takes a really long time

21 "A long time ___ …"

22 Up to this point

23 We all need it to live

24 "What ___ four wheels and flies?"

25 "Do ___ tell you!": 2 words

26 Positive answer

28 Suntan ___ (what you put on at the beach)

29 Area where a college is

31 "That's ___ fair!"

32 How a French person says the word at 26-Down

33 School groups that have "open houses": Abbreviation

34 Went over 75 miles per hour

35 That woman

36 "I Believe I ___ Fly" (R. Kelly song)

37 Like the numbers 3, 7, and 19

38 Female sheep

39 Athlete who gets paid

40 A self-centered person has a big one

41 It divides a ping-pong table in half

2

ACROSS

1 "The King of ___" (Michael Jackson)
4 Little round vegetable
7 Drink that's often "sweetened" or "unsweetened"
10 Square section of a window
11 Not feeling well
12 Sixty-minute periods: Abbreviation
13 Al Gore, for example: 2 words
16 "Planet of the ___"
17 Card that can be worth 1 or 11
18 Continent that contains Mount Everest
19 The newsman's name on "The Mary Tyler Moore Show"
20 A man might wear one with a suit
21 Guide a car
22 Prince William, to Prince Charles
23 Dessert with a crust
24 City in Montana
27 "I've ___ an idea!"
28 Not cooked at all
31 "Peekaboo, ___ you!": 2 words
32 Opposite of "peace"
33 The North ___ (where Santa lives)
34 Where the person at 13-Across works: 3 words
37 Two times five
38 "You ___ My Sunshine"
39 4 goes ___ 12 three times
40 1999 and 2000, for example: Abbreviation
41 Not "no" or "maybe"
42 Color Easter eggs

DOWN

1 Walked back and forth nervously
2 Dollar bills that show George Washington
3 Energy and enthusiasm
4 Slice
5 "What ___ could I do?"
6 "___ Baba and the Forty Thieves"
7 The ones over here
8 Bert's roommate on "Sesame Street"
9 "When you wish upon ___ …": 2 words
10 Old King Cole called for it

13 Container that stores wine

14 Weather that would spoil a picnic

15 August 7, 1999, for example

20 It's at the end of the foot

21 Stop standing

22 Food that contains meat and vegetables

23 Very tiny hole in the skin

24 Itty-___ (very tiny)

25 Person who shows people to their seats

26 People between 12 and 20 years old

27 Bill ___ (the president of Microsoft)

28 Path that a mail carrier travels

29 Not to mention

30 ___ Willie Winkie

32 Some fences are made of it

33 ___ express (old mail delivery system)

35 It's scattered around in barns

36 Put something where it wouldn't be found

3

ACROSS

1 "___ see …"
5 A dollar is equal to 100 of them: Abbreviation
8 Last word in a prayer
12 Many: 2 words
13 ___ de Janeiro (city in Brazil)
14 Cab
15 Say that something isn't true
16 Holiday ___ (name of a hotel)
17 "I smell ___!": 2 words
18 Chemistry or biology: Abbreviation
19 Send a letter on a computer: Hyphenated
21 It cools down a drink
22 Kind of steak: Hyphenated
24 How much a jewel might weigh
26 Stuck in a ___
27 "___, humbug!"
28 With less clothing on
30 It might be made of barbed wire

32 The Chicago White ___
33 Opposite of "attract"
35 "What ___ you talking about?"
37 "Do ___ others …"
39 Animal with udders
40 Verbal
41 Dr. Frankenstein's assistant
42 Gorilla
43 What you sit at, in school
44 Dial ___ (phone sound)
45 Miles ___ hour
46 Changes the color of one's hair

DOWN

1 Boys
2 Vote into office
3 Singer of "Another Sad Love Song": 2 words
4 Place where pigs live
5 "___ does not pay"
6 Rock singer ___ Turner
7 ___ the Hedgehog

8 One ___ time: 2 words

9 Singer of "Dreamlover": 2 words

10 Precise

11 Nick at ___ (cable channel)

19 Go inside

20 Tag on a piece of clothing

23 Your and my

25 Moved quickly

28 Kind of drum

29 Briefly review something again

30 Not as many

31 Use one end of a pencil

32 Diamonds or spades, for example

34 The head of the Catholic Church

36 Animals with antlers

38 State that borders California: Abbreviation

40 Weird

4

ACROSS

1 A vitamin or an aspirin, for example
5 Furniture in the living room
9 "It's ___ your own good!"
12 The dog in "Garfield"
13 A mile is a ___ of length
14 Type of bread
15 Playground game: 2 words
17 Kind of tree
18 Uncle ___ (symbol of the U.S.A.)
19 Place where you might go fishing
21 "Who ___ that masked man?"
24 ___-tac-toe
26 A rectangle has four of them
29 Spin like ___: 2 words
31 Noisy kind of dancing
33 Bird that's a symbol of peace
34 A car's dashboard usually has one
36 Evil
38 "You've ___ your match!"
39 Insects at picnics

41 Cry
43 Part of the body near the middle
45 Playground game
50 Game with "Wild Draw 4" cards
51 It's a "Great" 19-Across
52 "That's terrible!": 2 words
53 Popular clothing store
54 A saxophone player uses one
55 Clark ___ (Superman's secret identity)

DOWN

1 Peas come in one
2 What the bride says at a wedding: 2 words
3 Covering on a jar
4 Insects have six of them
5 Hand in
6 Out ___ limb (in danger): 2 words
7 Put gas in the tank
8 Book of maps
9 ___ of the press (part of the First Amendment)
10 Olive ___ (Popeye's girlfriend)

11 Rock band that features Michael Stipe
16 Have a meal
20 Baby goat
21 The Revolutionary ___
22 "I'm ___ loss for words!": 2 words
23 Cola: 2 words
25 It might drive a person from the airport
27 New Year's ___
28 Complete collection
30 It's knocked down in bowling
32 Didn't fail

35 Not this or that
37 "Snow White" character
40 Really annoyed
42 It can be checked out of a library
43 Embrace
44 "… and pretty maids all ___ row": 2 words
46 Kind of dessert
47 Word that starts a lot of titles
48 TV channel that shows current events
49 Like most summer days

5

ACROSS

1 "For ___ a jolly good fellow …"
4 Sick
7 Hurry up
11 Kind of grain
12 Take a look at
13 The biggest continent
14 Collectible toys of the 1980s
17 What some people do when they don't get their way
18 ___ and downs
19 Opposite of "true"
21 ___ and hers
22 Month that contains Mother's Day
25 Busy as ___: 2 words
26 Some cans are made from it
27 Part of a highway
28 Top color on a rainbow
29 Unhappy
30 Rock groups
31 Tyrannosaurus ___
32 Where your funny bones are
33 Collectible toys of the 1990s: 2 words

38 "Green ___ and Ham"
39 "___ Baba and the Forty Thieves"
40 Be in debt
41 How much medicine you're supposed to take at once
42 Number of years in a decade
43 You catch butterflies with it

DOWN

1 Sizzling
2 You might pierce it
3 Connected papers together, in a way
4 A single magazine
5 Went out of the room
6 A sign of the Zodiac
7 Wheelchair entrances
8 Avails oneself of
9 ___ Lancelot (famous knight)
10 Possesses
15 It smells
16 Destroy

19 Not near
20 Nickname of President Lincoln
21 Went where people couldn't find you
22 Huge house
23 What the symbol "&" means
24 "You bet!"
26 Kind of car that's often yellow
27 Young sheep

29 Sight or hearing, for example
30 It's in your head
31 Cloths that people dust with
32 Ready, willing, and ___
33 Place for a nap
34 A vain person has a big one
35 Have breakfast
36 Female sheep
37 "Ready, ___, go!"

6

ACROSS

1 Birds that are often blue
5 Close friend
8 What omelets are made of
12 Black-and-white cookie
13 Put frosting on a cake
14 Kind of song sung in a 29-Across
15 Alexander Graham ___ (inventor of the telephone)
16 It's used to catch fish
17 Pressed the doorbell
18 Not first
20 State where Nashville is: Abbreviation
22 Opposite of tall
24 That girl
25 Dachshund or Dalmatian
28 "___ now, brown cow?"
29 "Carmen" is a famous one
31 ___ ball (the white ball in billiards)
32 What nodding your head means
33 Truck that moves furniture
34 Intelligent
36 Now and ___

38 Strap that's used to control a horse
39 "Go away!"
41 Animal that's like a big monkey
43 Use a keyboard
46 Put clothes away in the closet
47 What a boy will become
48 You have ten of them on your body
49 You have two of them on your body
50 An aardvark might eat one
51 Make a noise with your thumb and middle finger

DOWN

1 Career
2 "You ___ My Sunshine"
3 National park in Wyoming
4 ___ eclipse
5 Half of a quart
6 Card that's worth 1 or 11
7 Q, for example
8 Deserve

9 National park in Arizona: 2 words

10 ___ rummy (card game)

11 Droop

19 Appliance in the kitchen

21 Get chalk off the blackboard

22 Afraid to meet new people

23 A gardener uses it to attack weeds

24 Bird on a farm

26 Your and my

27 Obtain

30 Country that has a famous canal

35 Baseball catchers wear them

37 Big pigs

38 Money paid to the landlord

39 That woman

40 Farmers might put it into a bale

42 Frying ___

44 "The Princess and the ___"

45 Power that psychics say they have: Abbreviation

7

ACROSS

1 Cain's brother, in the Bible
5 Put ___ show: 2 words
8 "___ Loves You" (Beatles song)
11 David Copperfield does it
13 Scary rodent
14 Slinky or yo-yo, for example
15 It's sometimes on top of a Christmas tree
16 Long ___ (way back when)
17 Animal that mates with a ram
18 "Yield" or "Don't Walk," for example
20 Average score on a golf course
22 Alphabet's beginning
25 One of the girls in "Little Women"
26 Allows
29 Beverage that uses ice cream: 3 words
33 Go from one house to a new one
34 ___ Montana (famous football player)
35 Secret agent
36 Finish

38 Its capital is Salt Lake City
40 Candy ___
42 ___ Baba
44 Dish of tossed vegetables
48 What metal is called when it has just been mined
49 Hanukkah's month: Abbreviation
50 Copy a drawing
51 Place for napping
52 Observe
53 Changes the color of one's hair

DOWN

1 "Today I ___ man" (bar mitzvah boy's phrase): 2 words
2 Forbid
3 It might be hard-boiled
4 Doesn't tell the truth
5 Beverage at breakfast: 2 words
6 Old horse
7 Above
8 Music systems
9 "___ do you do?"

10 Where the pupil is
12 Go up a ladder
19 "___ whiz!"
21 100 percent
22 It's attached to the shoulder
23 Ghosts say it
24 ___ wagon (pioneer's transportation)
27 Sound that a woodpecker makes
28 Where a pig lives
30 Bill that has a portrait of Alexander Hamilton on it
31 Decay
32 Big dinner
37 Fathers
39 Really tough
40 ___ for apples (what you might do on Halloween)
41 "___ you serious?"
43 Robert E. ___ (general in the Civil War)
45 Put down
46 Good card to have in the game 21
47 ___ Moines (capital of Iowa)

8

ACROSS

1 "Yo-ho-ho and a bottle of ___"
4 Person who makes up rhymes
8 Unit of computer memory
12 Every once ___ while: 2 words
13 "Hey, what's the big ___?"
14 There might be one on the side of a staircase
15 Game with deeds and Chance cards
17 "Excuse me ..."
18 That girl
19 Pocket fuzz
21 Word you use during long division
24 You make soup in it
25 Sound of a ray gun
28 Rescue a car
29 Constellations are made up of them
31 Animal that gives birth to lambs
32 "___ was saying ...": 2 words
33 Baby goat
34 Vehicle that can handle rough terrain
35 Part of the leg
37 Sticky stuff
39 ___ Rose (famous ballplayer who was banned from baseball)
41 Game with tiles and Triple Letter Squares
46 "And they lived happily ___ after"
47 Fix mistakes in writing
48 Younger version of the word at 3-Down
49 "What ___ we thinking?"
50 Part of a camera
51 Take someone to court

DOWN

1 It surrounds a basketball net
2 Numero ___ (#1)
3 Guy
4 Frosty the Snowman had one
5 Bad smell
6 Long, skinny fish
7 Jonathan ___ Thomas
8 Ingredient in some cereals that has a lot of fiber
9 Game with dice and "small straights"
10 Make a knot

11 Kind of tree
16 Exclamation like "Aha!"
20 "___ none of your business!"
21 "Give ___ chance!": 2 words
22 1, 2, and 3: Abbreviation
23 Game with colored circles and a spinner
24 Lily ___ (what a frog sits on)
26 In ___ of (impressed by)
27 ___ rally
29 Glide down a snowy mountain

30 Shiny stuff on a Christmas tree
34 What someone does for a living
36 In this spot
37 Smile broadly
38 Grains that horses eat
39 Long seat in church
40 Christmas ___ (December 24)
42 Letters between B and F
43 Ammo for a toy gun
44 "Skip to My ___"
45 Private ___ (detective)

9

ACROSS

1 Insect that lives in a hill
4 Opposite of skinny
7 Sack
10 Game that ends in a tie score
11 Not wild
12 A long time ___
13 Timesaver in the living room: 2 words
16 A half plus a half
17 Drenches with water
18 Part of a parka
19 Parts of quarts: Abbreviation
20 ___ and outs
21 Put in the mail
22 Covered in frost
23 "What's the reason?"
24 Adorable
26 Little round vegetable
27 Animal that moos
30 "That's terrible!": 2 words
31 Smack in the face
32 King Kong was one
33 Timesaver in the kitchen: 2 words
36 Sick
37 Walking stick
38 Some people pay it every month
39 Peg that golfers use
40 Explosive stuff: Abbreviation
41 Suffix after "host" or "lion"

DOWN

1 "You ___ the boss of me!"
2 Barry, Harry, and Larry
3 16-Across plus 16-Across
4 Truthful bits of information
5 Famous ___ (brand of cookie)
6 3-Down times five
7 The Red ___ (Snoopy's enemy)
8 "Merry Christmas to all, and to all ___ night!": 2 words
9 Valuable metal
10 Let something fall

11 ___-weeny
14 More than once
15 All those people
21 Rectangle or square
22 "Believe ___ not!":
2 words
23 Make something with a
loom
24 Country in South
America
25 Member of the
family

26 It grows in a garden
27 Homes for bats
28 Unlocks
29 Left the room
30 Leave out
31 What the Ugly
Duckling turned
into
34 Halloween's month:
Abbreviation
35 State that's next to
Idaho: Abbreviation

10

ACROSS

1 Owns
4 Everest and McKinley: Abbreviation
7 A billy or a nanny
11 Ginger ___
12 An object used in a play
14 Short word for what goes into weapons
15 "I'm very impressed!"
16 Circle above an angel's head
17 Infant
18 "I ___ this would happen!"
20 Prefix for "byte" or "phone"
22 "For ___ a Jolly Good Fellow"
23 Hold with the hand
25 Another name for an Academy Award
27 The Dynamic ___ (Batman and Robin)
28 Polite thing to call a man
29 Stainless ___
31 You might call it during a coin toss

34 "Halt! ___ goes there?"
35 Pasta similar to rigatoni
37 Mammals that fly
39 "Darn it!"
41 "Have a ___ day!"
43 What Wayne says in "Wayne's World"
44 ___ code (numbers in parentheses in a phone number)
45 They have long antlers
46 Adam and ___
47 Really annoying person
48 Recipe measurement: Abbreviation
49 Use needle and thread

DOWN

1 Bird of prey
2 Get ___ with (like)
3 It runs under the city
4 Abbreviation on a speed limit sign
5 People bounce on it for fun
6 The bottom of the foot
7 Talk a lot
8 City in Nebraska

9 "... for ___ waves of grain"

10 Santa delivers them

13 People bounce on them for fun: 2 words

19 Walk into a river

21 Where China and India are

24 Canal in Egypt

26 Place for an infant

29 Let other people use your things with you

30 Carries

32 Highways are divided into them

33 You can cook on it

34 Cover up a gift

36 What a pinball machine says if you treat it badly

38 Food with meat and vegetables in it

40 Used a chair

42 Mind reader's ability, supposedly: Abbreviation

11

ACROSS

1 Part of the ear where you put an earring
5 Tie a shoe
9 It can cool you off in the summer
12 "Now ___ me down to sleep ...": 2 words
13 "I met ___ with seven wives": 2 words
14 ___ de Janeiro, Brazil
15 ___ Tyson (famous boxer who bit an opponent's ear)
16 Part of a three-piece suit
17 It can end the words "count" and "priest"
18 Cain and Abel's mother
19 Part of a robe
20 ___ child (kid with no brothers or sisters)
21 Fix a magazine story
23 Meeting where people try to talk to ghosts
25 A limerick, for example
27 "Get ___ the program!"
28 Fake hair for a man
30 Part of a barn where hay is stored
32 Funny people
33 Snoozes

35 Stimpy's pal, in cartoons
37 "___ Yankee Doodle Dandy": 2 words
38 "In ___ of emergency, break glass"
39 ___ and dandy
40 "Have we ___ somewhere before?"
41 High cards, usually
42 More or ___
43 Athlete who gets paid
44 A karate student wears one
45 Takes advantage of

DOWN

1 Jell-O flavor
2 Salad ingredient, perhaps
3 Common side dish: 2 words
4 Hole in a needle
5 What a volcano shoots
6 Make ___ of things (foul things up): 2 words
7 Kidney-shaped nut
8 It can end the word "differ"

1	2	3	4		5	6	7	8		9	10	11
12					13					14		
15					16					17		
18				19					20			
	21		22			23		24				
		25			26		27					
	28					29		30			31	
32				33		34			35			36
37			38					39				
40			41					42				
43			44					45				

9 Common side dish: 2 words

10 What a bride walks down

11 Like a snoop

19 A ___ in the right direction

20 "Hold ___ your hat!": 2 words

22 Papers given to people who lend money: Abbreviation

24 Is sick

26 "Dennis the ___"

28 Stopwatch, for example

29 It holds up a painter's canvas

31 Stressed out

32 Cowardly person

34 Gnat or flea, for example

36 Suffix for "quick" or "thick"

38 Vehicle that people "hail" when they want it

39 Sickness that's common in winter

12

ACROSS

1 "___ tell you what …"
4 Word on a light switch
7 Points found on some wire fences
12 Drink that's sometimes "iced"
13 Bath place
14 "Take ___ at this!": 2 words
15 It's celebrated in late winter: 3 words, abbreviation
18 "___ Got the Whole World in His Hands"
19 Name for a lion
20 "Could you do me a ___?"
23 Mayonnaise holder
24 A trapeze artist might fall into it
27 Run ___ from home
28 Short sleep
29 Word on a valentine
30 Room that might have a TV in it
31 Do some needlework
32 Noisemaker on an ambulance
33 The Civil ___
34 Music from Will Smith
35 It's celebrated in early spring: 3 words

42 A good employee might get one
43 Overweight
44 Ginger ___
45 Uses a keyboard
46 Commercials
47 What wrestlers wrestle on

DOWN

1 "___ up to you"
2 Permit
3 One time around the track course
4 Mammal that likes to play in water
5 Mink and ermine
6 "The X-Files" are supposed to be a part of this agency: Abbreviation
7 "The butcher, the ___, the candlestick maker"
8 Not to mention
9 Fishing pole
10 ___ constrictor (big snake)
11 It's up above us
16 Word a sailor says instead of "Hello!"
17 Applaud

20 Popular thing that doesn't last long

21 Amazement

22 Martin ___ Buren (former president)

23 Bone that enables you to chew

24 Word that comes after "neither"

25 She lived in the Garden of Eden

26 What X is equal to, in Roman numerals

28 Brand name of "soft" balls

29 You kiss with them

31 Department store events

32 Sprinkles a certain seasoning on food

33 Very smart

34 Street

35 Paintings and so forth

36 Give money to

37 Make a tear in

38 Three ___ kind (poker hand): 2 words

39 A beaver builds it

40 State next to Georgia: Abbreviation

41 Up to now

13

ACROSS

1 Some parents
5 They hold 20-Across
9 Worker for Santa
12 "I cannot tell ___":
2 words
13 Running track's
shape
14 Dessert that has a
crust
15 Go up
16 Say that something
isn't true
17 One of the tokens in
Monopoly
18 Barbie's boyfriend
19 Put something through
a fax machine
20 Yellow vegetable
21 Birds build them
23 What doctors give you
in order to prevent
diseases
25 "What do ___
think?"
26 Joan of ___ (famous
French woman)
27 Went back and forth like
a pendulum
29 Drink that's made from
apples
31 Word on a red sign

32 Not phony
34 What a basketball goes
through
36 Paddle
37 From ___ to riches
38 "___ Wonderful Life":
2 words
39 Chicago's state:
Abbreviation
40 Border
41 Ooze
42 Was ahead of everyone
else
43 Filthy place
44 ___ & Entertainment
(cable channel)

DOWN

1 Opposite of light
2 Creature from Mars
3 Fun place in Florida:
2 words
4 "I ___ what you
mean"
5 Spies use them to hide
their messages
6 Kitchen appliance
7 Rubber ___ (stretchy
things)
8 ___ as a fox

9 Fun place in Florida:
2 words
10 They don't tell the
truth
11 Houseplant that has
fronds
19 Astonish
20 What you pull to open a
parachute
22 Chicken noodle or
cream of broccoli
24 Winter weather
27 Like bread that's gotten
hard

28 A+, for example
29 Attaché ___ (things that
carry documents)
30 Button you press in a
bowling alley
31 What you plant flowers
in
33 Ingredients in a cake
recipe
35 Water faucets
37 Band that sang "Shiny
Happy People"
38 "This ___ stickup!":
2 words

ACROSS

1 "How long ___ this been going on?"
4 Grows older
8 Stay around for a while
12 It can end the words "insist" and "differ"
13 Han ___ (hero in "Star Wars")
14 "… ___ partridge in a pear tree": 2 words
15 "Many years ___ …"
16 Pizza topping
18 City in Nevada
20 Not as much
21 Have a snack
22 Fix
24 King of the ___ (schoolyard game)
26 Suffix for the word "hero"
27 Was introduced to someone else
28 "Star ___" (TV show with Captain Kirk)
30 Police cars have them on top
33 That lady
34 Grassy yard

36 Things in front of doors that say "Welcome"
38 Pizza topping
41 One of the Three Stooges
42 Region
43 Horse's pace that's between a walk and a run
44 New Year's ___
45 Depend
46 Does some stitching
47 Where lions live

DOWN

1 Listen to
2 Fury
3 Rock
4 What's left in a fireplace
5 The only soccer player who can use his hands
6 ___ Fudd (Bugs Bunny's chaser)
7 Cries
8 Armed conflict
9 "Touched by an ___" (TV series)

10 Perfect

11 Small pie

17 Person who works in a theater

19 Kid on "The Andy Griffith Show"

23 Joint near your foot

25 Thing

27 Small fish

28 "That's neither here nor ___"

29 Make someone go away

30 Said bad words

31 "A Boy ___ Charlie Brown"

32 Place for cooking

33 Practice boxing

35 Music, dance, painting, etc.

37 Looked at

39 "Crime does not ___"

40 "___ up to you"

15

ACROSS

1 Dog, cat, or hamster, for example
4 Emergency letters
7 Jewish religious leader
12 "I ___ you one!"
13 Wolf down
14 Tim ___ ("Home Improvement" star)
15 Comic strip by Charles Schulz
17 Football team in Detroit
18 Suffix for "heir"
19 "___ sesame!"
20 Walks in water
23 Word that Scrooge said
24 When the sun is out
27 ___ rain (ecology problem)
28 Miles ___ hour
29 Drink that's made in Napa Valley
30 Kind of toothpaste
31 What groceries are put into
32 You pull them out of a garden
33 It comes at the end of a restaurant meal
35 You need it for frying
36 Birds that fly in a V shape
38 Comic strip by Bill Amend
42 Monsters in fairy tales
43 Get older
44 "What ___ you talking about?"
45 Carries
46 ___ and reel
47 Ballpoint ___

DOWN

1 The sound a balloon makes
2 Female sheep
3 The Mad Hatter drank it
4 Dr. ___ (children's book author)
5 Some grains
6 Roads: Abbreviation
7 Character on "Happy Days"
8 Tell ___ (fib): 2 words
9 Comic strip by Chic Young
10 Big ___ (famous landmark in London)
11 Drive-___ (places where movies are watched from cars)
16 Require

19 It helps row a boat
20 What a dog's tail might do
21 "___ Ventura, Pet Detective"
22 Comic strip by Scott Adams
23 Plead
25 Hide-___-seek
26 Word of agreement
28 Good friend
29 "They ___ thataway!"
31 "___ you!" (reaction to a sneeze)

32 Polished the floor
34 "Peekaboo, ___ you!": 2 words
35 ___ stick (bouncy toy)
36 "You've ___ to be kidding"
37 What a conceited person has a lot of
38 Distant
39 Kind of music Queen Latifah makes
40 Raw metal
41 A dozen minus a pair

16

ACROSS

1 Against the ___ (illegal)
4 Read electronically
8 Scoop water out of a boat
12 "A long time ___ ..."
13 Mexican food
14 Tickle Me ___
15 Snakes
17 Mountains in Europe
18 Kids sometimes sit on Santa's ___
19 Music purchases, for short
20 "___ and the Tramp"
22 Wild pig
25 Money that's left for the waiter
28 "___ my pleasure"
29 Humorous
30 Part of a royal flush, in poker
31 It holds up a golf ball
32 Word said at the end of a prayer
33 The people who work on a boat
34 Tyrannosaurus ___
36 As easy as falling off a ___
37 What umbrellas protect you from
39 Not forward or backward
44 Like cars that aren't new
45 Hot thing in the kitchen
46 "Oh, give ___ home where the buffalo roam ...": 2 words
47 Kind of fish
48 Stoop down
49 Finish up

DOWN

1 ___ Vegas
2 How old you are
3 Big baseball event: 2 words
4 A single stair
5 Soup comes in it
6 Play a role
7 Digits: Abbreviation
8 Small round thing on a necklace, sometimes
9 Big baseball event: 2 words, hyphenated
10 Little devil
11 ___ Angeles
16 Take care of the bills
19 Go "boo-hoo"
20 Turned on a lamp

21 Had some food
22 ___ around (wander aimlessly)
23 Half of two
24 Raggedy ___ (famous doll)
26 Cubes in the freezer
27 Where people sit in church
29 Machine that can send documents over phone lines
33 Milk-giving animal
35 Finishes

36 Give money temporarily
37 ___ the wrong way (irritate)
38 "___ matter of fact ...": 2 words
39 Go "boo-hoo"
40 "___ Been Working on the Railroad"
41 Comfortable room of the house
42 Kind of money that's used in Japan
43 Not happy

17

ACROSS

1 Boxer's punches
5 Coolio's music
8 Big wooden pole on a ship
12 Words of understanding: 2 words
13 Suffix that means "most"
14 State that has a lot of Mormons
15 Disney movie
17 Not early
18 "What ___ doing here?": 2 words
19 Health resort
21 "___ the season to be jolly ..."
24 "Oh, what's the ___?" ("What difference does it make?")
26 Vegetable that makes you cry when you chop it
30 Stuff in a pen
31 Look without blinking
33 Number in a duo
34 Perhaps
36 Decay
37 Do what Betsy Ross was famous for doing
38 Commercials

40 Get ready to shoot a basketball
42 Not quite hot
45 Disney movie
50 Someone who lives in the Middle East
51 "___ got an idea!"
52 Final
53 Prefix for "colon" or "final"
54 Homer's neighbor on "The Simpsons"
55 Potatoes have them

DOWN

1 Brand of peanut butter
2 Red ___ beet: 2 words
3 "Boy Meets World" actor Savage
4 ___ good example (what a role model should do): 2 words
5 "I couldn't ___" ("I just had to do it")
6 "Do ___ say!": 2 words
7 School groups that have open houses: Abbreviation
8 Disney movie
9 One ___ time: 2 words

10 Got into a chair
11 Most commonly written word in English
16 Made other people laugh
20 Like something written in verse
21 Tiny ___ (character in "A Christmas Carol")
22 "Never ___ million years!": 2 words
23 Where clouds are
25 Hearing organ
27 "___ been real!" ("I've had fun!")

28 Homophone of "oh"
29 At this moment
32 Sounded like a lion
35 Disney movie
39 ___ guards (protection for soccer players)
41 Stubborn animal
42 The past tense of "is"
43 "We ___ the World"
44 Male sheep
46 New Year's ___
47 Put down
48 Ending for "Japan" or "Vietnam"
49 Roads: Abbreviation

18

ACROSS

1 Villain in "The Lion King"
5 It's near your waist
8 What a spider spins
11 Triangle or trapezoid
12 Portland's state: Abbreviation
13 Pie ___ mode: 2 words
14 Bedsheet material
15 Werewolf or vampire
17 They invade picnics
18 Famous male doll
19 Quick kiss
20 Vegetable that comes in a pod
21 ___ conditioning
22 Line you make in your hair
23 Not first
25 What Old MacDonald had
26 ___ 'n' roll
27 Light brown
28 Small magical being
31 Go sightseeing
32 Neat as a ___
33 Run away from
34 He had "new clothes" in a famous story
36 By yourself
37 Southern general Robert E. ___
38 Number that changes on your birthday
39 Makes repairs
40 ___ Angeles
41 Indicate "yes" with your head
42 Throw a football

DOWN

1 Polish
2 Juicy fruits
3 Big hairy animals
4 Stimpy's cartoon pal
5 Bart Simpson's father
6 Get wrinkles out of clothes
7 It contains ink
8 Juicy fruits
9 Vote into office
10 The outside of a tree
11 Hit with an open hand

16 Practice boxing
18 Box that contains the parts for a model car
21 Pose a question
22 "Peter ___"
24 Measure of land
25 It can cool down a room
26 "___ and Juliet"
27 Exhausted
29 Gives temporarily

30 Extra costs
31 William ___ (legendary archer who shot an apple off his son's head
32 ___ stick (toy you hop on)
33 Bug that annoys dogs
35 Sprinted
36 Part of a fancy stereo system

19

ACROSS

1 Throw lightly
5 It dispenses money: Abbreviation
8 Sickness in the winter
11 Indian of Peru
12 "Give ___ break!": 2 words
13 Stumble
14 Sitcom of the 1990s
16 Fixes a squeaky hinge
17 Light brown
18 Ready to be picked and eaten
20 Until now: 2 words
23 Silver-colored metal
24 The Chicago Bears' group: Abbreviation
27 Part of the head
28 "Eight ___ a-milking ..."
30 What batteries eventually do
31 Baseball pitcher's statistic: Abbreviation
32 The supposed ability to read minds: Abbreviation
33 "___ trouble at all!": 2 words
35 Put in order

37 It follows "lemon" and "Gator" in drink names
38 Brand of bug spray
40 Sitcom of the 1990s
45 ___ tea (summer drink)
46 Tree that grows from an acorn
47 Steals from
48 The P of MPH
49 Peter, Paul, and Nick, for example: Abbreviation
50 Kill flies

DOWN

1 "___ the season to be jolly ..."
2 "We're number ___!"
3 ___-fi (kind of movie)
4 Rudolph the Red-Nosed Reindeer's boss
5 The last word of a hymn
6 You call someone on it: Abbreviation
7 Capital of Spain
8 Sitcom of the 1990s
9 "___ Abner" (comic strip)
10 ___ and downs
13 Spinning toy

15 "The ___ in the Dell"
19 Where people bring their pets during bad weather
20 Observe
21 Boat rower
22 Sitcom of the 1990s
23 The ___ of the iceberg
25 It's on the back of a shark
26 Sign of the zodiac
29 Baseball team from Houston

34 Signs of sadness
36 Like numbers that aren't divisible by two
37 Forms a question
38 Tear up
39 Card that beats a king
41 A single grain
42 At this time
43 The Chicago Bulls' group: Abbreviation
44 At the end of a word, it means more than "-er"

20

ACROSS

1 Makes knots
5 Place for a baby
9 Move fast, like lightning
12 Kind of self-defense
14 Country with a famous canal
15 Did as you were told
16 Metal used to make cans
17 It's sometimes worth more than a king
18 Places where scientists work
21 Young woman, in slang
23 Leader of the Catholic Church
27 "You ___ here" (words on a mall map)
28 Pie ___ mode (pie with ice cream): 2 words
29 Come in first
30 Food that has meat and vegetables in it
32 Bone in the chest
33 You can ride downhill on it
34 "A long time ___, in a galaxy far, far, away …"
36 Munch on
38 Music system for the home

41 Tribe that Geronimo belonged to
45 Last name of the fictional detective Sherlock
46 ___ on (depends on)
47 Sweet potatoes
48 What Aladdin rubbed

DOWN

1 Measurement in a recipe: Abbreviation
2 "Give ___ rest!": 2 words
3 Ending for "north" or "south"
4 Chairs
5 Nasty person
6 ___ of light
7 Suffix for "meteor"
8 Garden plot
10 "What ___ doing here?": 2 words
11 Australian animals
12 Australian animal: 2 words
13 Easy as ___
18 ___ Vegas, Nevada

19 Museums show it

20 Spelling ___ (school competition)

22 Boxer known as "The Greatest"

24 Bird that comes out at night

25 As American as apple ___

26 "Dead ___" (street sign)

31 Heats

33 Delay

35 "Golly!"

37 Kind of animal Tarzan hung out with

38 Not eager to meet new people

39 Come ___ conclusion (decide): 2 words

40 Kind of tree

42 Organization that hires spies: Abbreviation

43 It's at the bottom of a pants leg or skirt

44 Supposedly, it's a "sixth sense": Abbreviation

21

ACROSS

1 Treasure hunters need one
4 Sounds made by ewes
8 Moms' husbands
12 Its capital is Montgomery: Abbreviation
13 Curved part of the foot
14 Not closed
15 Neither this ___ that
16 Have supper
17 Soft drink
18 Bills with George Washington on them
20 Bambi was one
22 Take a small drink
23 Troll, in fairy tales
25 A field goal is kicked between these
27 Attempt
28 Polite thing to call a man
29 ___ Butler (character in "Gone With the Wind")
31 Poisonous stuff that comes from snakes
33 This woman
34 Where you live
36 "X marks the ___"
38 The Leaning Tower of ___
40 Barbed ___ fence
42 Tool used in the garden
43 Turn over ___ leaf: 2 words
44 "Or ___!" (part of a threat)
45 Suffix for "lion"
46 Pinocchio had a long one
47 Movie spool
48 "Ready, ___, go!"

DOWN

1 "Look, ___ hands!": 2 words
2 "You've come ___ way": 2 words
3 ( )
4 Evil
5 "Take ___ on the Reading" (Monopoly card): 2 words
6 Teenager's skin problem
7 Woolly animal

8 One of the Seven Dwarfs
9 ' ' ' ' '
10 Stores where you can buy sandwiches
11 "___, crackle, pop"
19 Tender, like a throat
21 Thorny flower
24 Story about Greek gods
26 The Seven Deadly ___
29 Big African animal, for short
30 Rapunzel was locked up in one
31 Poem
32 Large Canadian animal
33 C-___ (cable channel that shows Congress)
35 5,280 feet
37 Quiz
39 Sense of wonder and amazement
41 Electric ___ (snaky fish)

22

ACROSS

1 ___ eagle (American symbol)
5 Not good
8 What you fill a bird feeder with
12 "Believe ___ not!": 2 words
13 Word that's shouted at a bullfight
14 Square part of a window
15 Some kids collect them: 2 words
18 Peace's opposite
19 Boy
20 Owns
23 Things that attempt to sell products
25 Tattles
29 On the peak of
31 Depressed
33 Canvas thing on a boat
34 Where Houston is
36 Marry
38 Secret agent
39 Answer to an addition problem
41 Your lungs need it
43 What quarterbacks play in: 2 words

50 One of the five Great Lakes
51 A score of 3 to 3, for example
52 Place for a pet canary
53 Not sick
54 That girl
55 Side of a knife

DOWN

1 A baby wears it during meals
2 "I'm ___ loss for words!": 2 words
3 ___ Angeles
4 Made a sketch
5 Two-by-fours
6 "___ aboard!"
7 "The Farmer in the ___"
8 One of the four card suits
9 In one ___ and out the other
10 Go off the deep ___
11 ___ Moines, Iowa
16 Sheep's sound
17 Garfield is one
20 Head covering

1	2	3	4	■	5	6	7	■	8	9	10	11
12				■	13			■	14			
15			16				17					
■		18			■	19				■	■	■
20	21	22	■	23		24		■	25		26	27	28
29			30	■	31		32	■	33			
34				35	■	36		37	■	38		
■		39		40	■	41		42	■	■	■	
43	44	45			46				47	48	49
50			■	51			■	52			
53			■	54			■	55			

21 Swallowed
22 The Boston Red ___
24 Carpenter's cutter
26 ___ Vegas
27 It might get chapped
28 Sneaky, like a fox
30 Chalk-like crayon
32 Person who works in a casino
35 Vehicle that shoots torpedoes, for short
37 Use a shovel

40 School subject
42 The Indianapolis 500 is one
43 Not many
44 What miners try to find
45 Black fuel
46 Tell a whopper
47 Angry
48 "Which came first, the chicken or the ___?"
49 Observe

ACROSS

1 Sticky substances that come out of maple trees
5 ___ and far between (rare)
8 "The ___ in the Hat"
11 What a detective finds
12 Part of the foot
13 Ginger ___
14 Ready, willing, and ___
15 Remove from office
16 ___ the knot (get married)
17 You might ride to school in one
18 ___ hoop (kind of toy)
19 Insects that buzz
20 ___ badge (what a Boy Scout earns)
22 Find out new things in school
24 Stuff in a fireplace after a fire
25 Truck that moves furniture
26 Sharp and biting, like autumn weather
28 Fight
31 Stuff with fiber that's in healthy cereals

32 Not evens
34 Old horse
36 Tree with hard wood
37 Black-and-white cookie
38 Ben Franklin flew one with a key on it
39 "___ Been Working on the Railroad"
40 Have on, as a shirt
41 Thing
42 Had followers
43 Young man
44 Places where lions live

DOWN

1 It forms over a cut
2 Photo ___ (place to paste pictures)
3 Throbbing that you can feel near your wrist
4 Take a look at
5 Not fair, in baseball
6 Country in Central America: 2 words
7 Not dry
8 Provide the food for a party

9 Someone who flies in a flying saucer

10 Pegs used on a golf course

12 Country in Asia: 2 words

18 Sound a snake makes

19 Sound a firecracker makes

21 It can spoil a picnic

23 What Dumbo flapped in order to fly

26 Atlanta baseball player

27 Gathered the leaves in the yard

29 Bring together

30 Devoured

31 Put in hot water

33 Not alive

35 Jewels

37 Bird that hoots

38 Someone who's not a grownup yet

24

ACROSS

1 Movie about a pig that wanted to be a sheepdog
5 Curly, like hair
9 Precious stone
12 "I smell ___!" ("Something is suspicious!"): 2 words
13 Big test
14 Word that can go before "lobe" or "ring"
15 Money you owe someone else
16 How much a dime is worth: 2 words
18 "You bet!"
20 Middle ___ (when someone isn't really young or really old)
21 Be a thief
23 Pump ___ (lift weights)
27 Hold tightly
30 What the bride and groom say: 2 words
31 They hold money and valuable papers
33 Happy ___ clam: 2 words
34 Bad smell
36 Opening in a fence
37 Lay out in the sun
38 Magazine with Alfred E. Neuman

40 "___ was saying …": 2 words
42 Cold drink: 2 words
47 Noisemaker in a car
50 It comes after "neither"
51 Mother ___ (kids' game): 2 words
52 "Hold ___ your hats!": 2 words
53 Billboards
54 Drove faster than the law allows
55 Animals that wear a yoke

DOWN

1 Terrible
2 "You ___ the Sunshine of My Life"
3 People born between 1946 and 1965: 2 words
4 Suffix for "disk" or "major"
5 Damp
6 Hatchet
7 Lucy ___ Pelt (character in "Peanuts")
8 One place to go to the gym: Abbreviation
9 People born in the 1960s and 1970s: 2 words

10 "You are what you ___"

11 Wife's title: Abbreviation

17 What a chicken lays

19 Brother's sibling, for short

21 ___ Grande (river in Texas)

22 Weird

24 Dusting cloth

25 "This is the chance ___ lifetime!": 2 words

26 You need one in order to play badminton

28 "A mind ___ terrible thing to waste": 2 words

29 You fry bacon in it

32 Large body of water

35 Not cooked

39 They hold back rivers

41 "Go away!"

42 ___ good mood (happy): 2 words

43 Food fish

44 Poke someone on the shoulder

45 Homophone of "I"

46 Get ___ of (eliminate)

48 Highway: Abbreviation

49 Prefix for "sense" or "stop"

ACROSS

1 Big crowd
4 Drink that contains caffeine
7 Raises up
12 Kwik-E-Mart worker on "The Simpsons"
13 Like the numbers 3, 11, and 19
14 Really love
15 Woman who is half fish
17 Noisy thing on a fire truck
18 ___ Frank (famous diary writer)
19 Half of twenty
21 The ___ Sea (body of water bordering Israel)
22 Celebrity
24 Short swim
26 Roads and avenues: Abbreviation
27 Command to a dog
29 ___ office (place to mail letters)
31 "Do ___ say!": 2 words
33 Diamond or ruby, for example
35 Makes a ditch
37 Singer who used to be married to Sonny Bono
39 Money left for a waitress
41 Got bigger
43 Bees make it
45 Not in any place
47 Bert and ___ ("Sesame Street" friends)
48 Part of the foot
49 Woman in the Garden of Eden
50 People in charge of colleges
51 Pronoun for a woman
52 ___ Flanders (character on "The Simpsons")

DOWN

1 Baby's first word, sometimes
2 Unlocks
3 Crayola color: 2 words
4 "One ___ customer": 2 words
5 Make changes in an article
6 Did sums
7 ___ Vegas, Nevada

8 "___ it!" (successful shout): 2 words
9 Crayola color: 2 words
10 "Trick or ___"
11 Puts in the mail
16 Hamburger or chicken, for example
20 Little bite
23 Old piece of cloth
25 It contains peas
28 So far
30 Make an "Oh well!" sound

31 Felt sore all over
32 Area next to the ocean
34 After-dinner ___ (breath-freshening candies)
36 Start a game of tennis
38 Strap that controls a horse
40 Winnie-the-___
42 Plant that you don't want in a garden
44 Word of agreement
46 Pee-___ Herman

ACROSS

1 "The Red Planet"
5 One day ___ time: 2 words
8 Conversation
12 State where Toledo is
13 Stimpy's pal, in cartoons
14 Bart Simpson's sister
15 Bundles of paper
16 Enemy of Batman
18 "Just ___!" (Nike's slogan): 2 words
20 Use a needle and thread
21 Good buddy
23 Small bite
25 Enter data for a computer
29 People shout it to the bullfighter
30 Scrub really hard
32 Ending for "Japan"
33 Winter coat
35 Conclusion
36 One of the Bobbsey Twins
37 "Jack ___ Jill"
39 ___ Island (part of New York)
41 Enemy of Batman: 2 words, abbreviation
45 Uncle's wife
48 Part for an actor
49 They're not yeses
50 Chest protectors for babies
51 Graceful bird
52 Letters that signal for help
53 Metal fastener

DOWN

1 Clean the floor
2 "I knew it!"
3 Enemy of Batman
4 Just okay: Hyphenated
5 Ocean near the North Pole
6 Drink that's made from leaves
7 Little bugs
8 Bozo or Ronald McDonald
9 That guy
10 White ___ sheet: 2 words
11 Slightly brown
17 Strange person
19 Crazy
21 "___ Goes the Weasel"

22 ___ mode (with ice cream): 2 words

24 Edgar Allan ___ (famous writer)

26 Enemy of Batman

27 Country between Canada and Mexico: Abbreviation

28 Number of arms on a squid

31 "Don't do anything ___ I tell you to"

34 Girl's name

38 Comfortable rooms in houses

40 Captures

41 Abbreviation before a wife's name

42 Move a canoe

43 Miami's state: Abbreviation

44 Place to see animals

46 Shaquille O'Neal's group: Abbreviation

47 ¹/₃ of a tablespoon: Abbreviation

27

ACROSS

1 Piece of paper taken to the supermarket
5 Gorillas
9 Blind as a ___
12 China's continent
13 ___ Thomas (founder of Wendy's)
14 "Who do you think you ___?"
15 Detective in kids' books: 2 words
17 Robert E. ___ (famous general)
18 Make a hole
19 A ___ apple: 2 words
20 Plot
21 Animal with antlers
23 Pressure
25 Grand finale
27 It's used to make maple syrup
28 Where Topeka is
31 Not far away
34 Roly-___ (round)
35 Emotional state
37 Cindy-___ Who (girl in "How the Grinch Stole Christmas!")

39 State near Washington: Abbreviation
40 Detectives in kids' books: 2 words
42 Revolutions ___ minute
43 Got older
44 "___ upon a time …"
45 Have some food
46 Untidy place
47 They collect nectar

DOWN

1 ___ of Enchantment (New Mexico's nickname)
2 "Did you hear what ___?": 2 words
3 Burn a little bit
4 Tic-___-toe
5 Totals
6 Capital of France
7 Happenings
8 Do needlework
9 A game of pool uses 15 of them
10 Places
11 Someone between 12 and 20 years old

16 Materials that people knit with
20 ___ Le Pew (cartoon skunk)
22 "___, meeny, miny, moe ..."
24 One of the sons on "Home Improvement"
26 Harm
28 Asian country divided into "North" and "South"

29 Red ___ (danger signal)
30 Tender, achy spots
32 "Home ___" (Macaulay Culkin movie)
33 Rolls-___ (fancy car)
34 Vatican City religious leader
36 Evens' opponent in choosing up sides
38 ___ one's head (thinks)
40 Kind of meat
41 ___ for apples

ACROSS

1 Baseball hats
5 "___ your age and not your shoe size!"
8 What someone does for a living
11 Once more
13 An archer uses one
14 Go ___ diet (try to lose weight): 2 words
15 Fun ride: 2 words
18 Actress Thompson of "Caroline in the City"
19 Tell a fib
20 Doctors: Abbreviation
23 What might be served with potato chips
25 More recent
29 Sound that is made when a magician makes something disappear
31 "Do ___ disturb"
33 Like grass, in the morning
34 What to say when you answer the phone
36 ___ Sawyer (Huckleberry Finn's friend)
38 Black-and-yellow insect
39 ___ and downs
41 Used to be

43 Where you can ride the thing at 15-Across: 2 words
50 ___ and don'ts
51 ___ Rogers (famous cowboy)
52 "___ makes waste"
53 Be in debt
54 How old you are
55 All those people

DOWN

1 Automobile
2 "Give it ___!" ("Try it!"): 2 words
3 Good friend
4 Part of a window
5 Network that shows "Sabrina, the Teenage Witch"
6 Somewhat cold
7 Mark ___ ("Huckleberry Finn" author)
8 Write down quickly
9 Small number
10 Candy ___
12 Require
16 It can delay a baseball game
17 It can grow into a plant

20 55 ___ (speed limit): Abbreviation
21 Female deer
22 Note between fa and la
24 Cooking vessel
26 "Charlotte's ___"
27 Female sheep
28 Kind of bread
30 Winter sicknesses
32 Small city
35 Soap ___ (TV show that's on in the afternoon)
37 Algebra, for example
40 Weather problem

42 Small argument
43 "Much ___ About Nothing" (play by Shakespeare)
44 Cut the grass
45 "___ your imagination!"
46 Place for a contact lens
47 What's left after something burns
48 The path a mail carrier takes: Abbreviation
49 It fits into a lock

ACROSS

1 "___ in!" ("Eat up!")
4 Start of the alphabet
7 Light ___
11 Once ___ blue moon: 2 words
12 "Tra ___" (song sounds): 2 words
14 Thought
15 "Where the Wild Things Are" author: 2 words
18 Extra large or small, for example
19 Opposite of love
20 Ending for "Japan" or "Siam"
21 Look through a book
23 Sticky stuff used to make a road
24 Cherry-colored
25 Allow
27 Tear
29 Part of an atlas
32 Mauna ___ (volcano in Hawaii)
34 Has breakfast
37 Birmingham's state: Abbreviation
38 Big brass instrument

40 The ___ Piper
42 Author who wrote books about Busytown: 2 words
45 ___-ball (game where you roll balls)
46 Diamonds or hearts, for example
47 The first woman in the Bible
48 His and ___
49 ___ Vegas
50 ___ Moines, Iowa

DOWN

1 Turns down the lights
2 "The bombs bursting ___" (part of "The Star-Spangled Banner"): 2 words
3 Bandage material
4 Name of the prince in the movie "Aladdin"
5 Johann Sebastian ___ (famous composer)
6 Spike on the bottom of a soccer shoe
7 Container for coal

8 Part of a cow
9 Rent
10 Made a cake
13 "When you wish upon ___ ...": 2 words
16 Actual
17 Strange and spooky
22 One of the big airlines
26 Goes around and sees the sights
28 Father
29 Swampy area
30 "Share and share ___"

31 Indiana basketball player
33 Kareem ___-Jabbar (noted athlete)
35 Ready to go to sleep
36 Put food on the table
39 Where Russia and Japan are
41 They can change your hair color
43 "For ___ a jolly good fellow ..."
44 A quarter equals 25 of them: Abbreviation

ACROSS

1 Rival network of CBS
4 A fly might get trapped in one
7 Rock back and forth
11 Part of a traffic jam
12 "Who ___ to say?": 2 words
13 Department ___
14 The center part of a hurricane
15 Floor covering
16 Scavenger ___ (some party games)
17 It blocks the water in a river
19 Person from the Middle East, maybe
21 Ocean liner, for example
23 The answer to an addition problem
24 ___-Cone (frosty treat)
27 Really adorable: 4 words
31 ___ and outs
32 "___, humbug!"
33 Really dislike
34 The dog in "The Wizard of Oz"
35 Wager

36 "Happy Birthday ___": 2 words
39 ___ up (completely finish)
41 "___ an honor to meet you"
44 "You ___ my friend anymore!"
45 "Do you ___ what I mean?"
46 Have a debt
47 They catch butterflies
48 "___ my shorts!" (Bart Simpson's phrase)
49 Not later

DOWN

1 High card
2 Body of water similar to a gulf
3 They're on the screen when the movie is over
4 Toasty
5 Flightless bird from Australia
6 Very large: 4 words
7 Part of a ticket
8 Came in first place
9 You might put it in a frame

10 "I agree!"
13 Famous whale at Sea World
18 Hairy jungle animal
20 Move your hands over
21 Chemistry, for example: Abbreviation
22 Attila the ___
24 Train stop
25 "I'm ___ kidding!"
26 "___ of these days ..."
28 "Mad ___ You" (TV comedy)

29 Stopped standing up
30 Word that starts many titles
34 2000-pound weights
35 Red vegetable
36 Dark beige
37 Metal that's just been mined
38 Up to now
40 Word before "horse" or "shell"
42 Number of twins
43 Make clothing

31

ACROSS

1 "Wheel of Fortune" host ___ Sajak
4 It can help move a boat
7 Stuff in a museum
10 Boxer Muhammad ___
11 ___ de Janeiro
12 Money in Italy
14 It involves having wheels under your feet
18 The son on "The Cosby Show"
19 "___ no evil, hear no evil, speak no evil"
20 Soft drink
21 Rude, like back talk
23 Depressing
25 Droop down in the middle
26 ___ Diego, California
28 Heavy mist
30 ___ and don'ts
33 Pigs roll around in it
35 Tool that holds things together
39 Gobbles up
41 Mother
43 Location
44 It involves having wheels under your feet

47 Cole ___ (side dish made from cabbage)
48 Deli bread
49 Take someone to court
50 Private ___ (detective)
51 The Chicago White ___
52 Suffix for "host"

DOWN

1 Fractions of the whole thing
2 It means "hello" or "goodbye" in Hawaii
3 Shingles
4 Stuff that's dug out of the ground
5 Put on ___ (act like a snob)
6 People sometimes wear them after showering
7 State next to Mississippi: Abbreviation
8 Removes
9 Groups of three people
13 "Three Men ___ Baby" (movie comedy): 2 words
15 Defeat

16 It turns colors in the autumn
17 It can stop someone from talking
22 Thanksgiving vegetable
24 Friend of Sleepy and Bashful
27 Not feeling anything
29 Happy
30 ___ Moines
31 What acorns grow up to be
32 Not fresh any more
34 Entrances
36 Get out of bed
37 What waiters bring before meals
38 Sheets in a book
40 Command to Fido
42 Sandwich spread, for short
45 Female farm animal
46 Tyrannosaurus ___

32

ACROSS

1 Tear open
4 You pound them into the ground to anchor a tent
8 Fifty-yard dash, for example
12 ___ of a kind (unique)
13 Farm animals
14 "Now ___ me down to sleep ...": 2 words
15 Brownish color
16 Expensive automobile
18 Person who makes verses
20 "It's no ___!" ("It doesn't work!")
21 The American flag has 50 of them
23 School group: Abbreviation
24 Gave a meal to
27 What golfers aim for
28 That guy's
29 Fly high
30 Positive answer
31 Weather that makes it hard to see
32 Fragments
33 What we breathe
34 What new parents have to decide on
35 Expensive automobile: 2 words
39 Rip ___ Winkle
42 Come to a stop
43 Direction on a compass
44 What a vain person has
45 Finishes
46 Stick around
47 One of the primary colors

DOWN

1 Decay
2 ___ little while (soon): 2 words
3 Faraway people you write to: 2 words
4 The north and south ends of the Earth
5 The way out
6 Sapphire or ruby, for example
7 Hogs' noses
8 "___ and shine!"
9 ___ Baba
10 "You ___ do it!"
11 Where the pupil and cornea are
17 ___ Today (popular newspaper)

19 Its capital is Salem: Abbreviation
21 Bashful
22 Digit on the foot
23 Animal that gives us pork
24 Always
25 Consume
26 Medical workers: Abbreviation
28 They neigh and whinny
29 The butcher on "The Brady Bunch"
31 Physically ___ (in shape)

32 Birthday ___
33 ___ and crafts
34 Group that sends up space shuttles: Abbreviation
35 Pronoun for a girl
36 Peter ___ (boy who didn't want to grow up)
37 Not young
38 Popular pet
40 How many years old you are
41 Wynken, Blynken, and ___

ACROSS

1 Sinks downward
5 Supposed ability to read minds: Abbreviation
8 Cool ___ cucumber: 2 words
11 Sign above a door, sometimes
12 Thin as a ___
14 Corny joke
15 "If it ___ up to me …"
16 Zoo animal
18 "Planet of the ___"
20 ___ shoes (things a ballerina wears)
21 Not on
23 The square root of 100
25 They're sold by the dozen
29 TV alien from the planet Melmac
30 Stuffed-___ pizza
33 Big tree
34 Sandwich breads
36 Pekoe is a type of this
37 Baseball statistic: Abbreviation
38 Sam-___ (Dr. Seuss character): Hyphenated
41 Me, myself, ___: 2 words

43 Zoo animal
47 Too
50 "___ and improved"
51 Captain Hook's sidekick in "Peter Pan"
52 Cole ___ (common side dish)
53 Opposite of "live"
54 Put two and two together
55 Detest

DOWN

1 Join with stitches
2 The Tin Man carried one
3 Zoo animal
4 A ___ in the right direction
5 One end of a pencil
6 ___ Francisco
7 Movie star Brad ___
8 "Many years ___ …"
9 It comes out of maple trees
10 Ending for "orphan" or "percent"
13 Zodiac sign that comes after Cancer
17 Grant's opponent in the Civil War

19 "And others": Abbreviation
21 Paddle for a boat
22 Go up in a plane
24 Cashew or macadamia
26 Zoo animal
27 Talk and talk and talk
28 Water-___ (have fun on a lake)
31 "Please be ___" ("Get in your chairs")
32 Light brown color
35 Take a tiny drink of
39 Sounds the doctor tells you to make

40 One of the Berenstain Bears
42 Hundred-yard ___ (kind of race)
43 "___ of the Road" (Boyz II Men song)
44 Ring of flowers they give out in Hawaii
45 She gives birth to a lamb
46 Boy's name
48 Weekend day: Abbreviation
49 "I ___ you one!" ("I'm in your debt!")

34

ACROSS

1 They connect things to bulletin boards
6 Shoot ___ breeze (chat)
9 "___ to the World"
12 Expect
13 ___ and vinegar (salad dressing)
14 Ginger ___
15 Sharp and tangy
16 Crunchy snacks
18 Give a hand
20 Was in front of
21 Nickname of President Lincoln
23 Hearing organ
25 Cords
29 Animals that have calves
31 Peak
33 City in Nevada
34 Stand that an artist uses
36 Drink that sounds like a letter of the alphabet
38 Commercials
39 "It ___ a dark and stormy night"
41 Scheme
43 Crunchy snacks
47 What an active volcano may do
50 Word that can go in front of "glasses" or "lashes"
51 In a ___ (doing the same thing over and over)
52 Fix a shoelace that's come undone
53 ___ for mercy
54 "___ questions?"
55 One of the five senses

DOWN

1 "___-Mania" (cartoon show)
2 In ___ of (amazed by)
3 Crunchy snacks
4 Toy that's fun to fly
5 Go out of ___ (become less hip)
6 "Only one ___ customer": 2 words
7 Small mountain
8 ___ Fudd (character in "Bugs Bunny" cartoons)
9 The middle girl on "The Brady Bunch"
10 Not new
11 "That's right!"
17 Stinky smell

19 Give someone a ___ on the back

21 Good card to have in the card game war

22 ___ constrictor (kind of snake)

24 Start to get moldy

26 Crunchy snacks

27 The last part

28 Letters that form a cry for help

30 Stitched

32 ___ talk (what a coach gives the team)

35 ___ Ingalls Wilder ("Little House on the Prairie" writer)

37 Red ___ (danger signal)

40 Amaze

42 ___ code (part of a phone number)

43 What a spider makes

44 How a sailor says "yes"

45 Part of a table

46 Where a pig lives

48 The center of a cherry

49 What a golfer puts the ball on

ACROSS

1 ___-tac-toe
4 "What time ___?":
2 words
8 Small unit of weight
12 "What did ___ to
deserve this?": 2 words
13 Kind of self-defense
14 "How awful!": 2 words
15 It contains ink
16 Make a sweater
17 How you might order
fast food: 2 words
18 Not crazy
20 Just average:
Hyphenated
22 Room that might have a
TV in it
23 "The ___ Garden"
(classic kids' book)
25 Animal that has fawns
27 Casual talk
28 "___ lay me down to
sleep ...": 2 words
29 What a red traffic signal
means
30 Touch softly
32 "___ the only one?"
("Doesn't anyone
agree?"): 2 words

33 Try to kill flies
35 Messy person
37 Having a lot of
money
39 Just ___ (not much at
all): 2 words
41 State near Florida:
Abbreviation
42 Part of a crossword
43 "Saturday Night ___"
(TV show)
44 Catch, like a criminal
45 Collections
46 Joint in the leg
47 Not wet

DOWN

1 Amounts left for the
waiters
2 Bright thoughts
3 New England state
4 Letters between H and L
5 When it starts to get
dark
6 Really dumb person
7 Tater ___ (side dish)
8 "I've ___ it!" ("I know
what to do!")

9 New England state: 2 words

10 Make mad

11 It's in the night sky

19 Sound that comes back after you say it

21 Unpleasant smell

24 Sings like L.L. Cool J

26 Rams' mates

28 Someone who was born in a certain place

29 What a photographer tells you to do

30 Log ___ (where Abraham Lincoln grew up)

31 ___ eclipse

32 Curved parts of circles

34 What one-year-olds learn to do

36 Infant

38 "For ___ a jolly good fellow ..."

40 Peg used by a golfer

ACROSS

1 New York baseball player
4 Pie ___ mode: 2 words
7 Piece of silverware
12 What the O stands for in "I.O.U."
13 Grab
14 Instrument with 88 keys
15 Pay-___-view
16 Network that shows "Friends"
17 Showed a TV show again
18 Sound from a lion
20 Magazine that includes movie spoofs
21 It's on the side of an escalator
23 "Go ___!" ("Scram!")
25 ___-fi (books about aliens and such)
28 Like hand-me-downs
29 Its capital is Dover: Abbreviation
30 Little fight
31 Chocolate ___
32 Fizzy drink
33 Mr. Spock had pointy ones, on "Star Trek"
34 Long-lasting card game
35 Nasty
37 Desert animal with a hump
40 Opposite of "sell"
41 "___ not amused": 2 words
44 By oneself
45 Had some food
46 A vain person has a big one
47 Makes a plan
48 Word of agreement
49 Not high

DOWN

1 It's used to clean the floor
2 She's covered in wool
3 Kind of dog
4 ___ Sewell ("Black Beauty" author)
5 Kind of dog
6 Easy as ___
7 Word that can go after "hair" or "bug"
8 The ___ Piper of Hamelin

9 Paddle

10 Out ___ limb: 2 words

11 Prefix for "violent"

19 As ___ as the hills

20 Kind of dog

21 Give a massage

22 Stubborn ___ mule: 2 words

24 The middle of the work week: Abbreviation

25 Kind of dog

26 It might be in a garage

27 "___ not my problem"

30 The Caspian ___ (big body of water)

32 Store discounts

34 ___ away (disappeared)

36 Buds on a potato

37 Hat with a team logo

38 "That's ___, folks!"

39 Cow's sound

40 Small body of water

42 Long ___ (in the past)

43 Cut the grass

ACROSS

1 It forms on top of a wound
5 Janitors use them
9 Tiny ___ ("A Christmas Carol" character)
12 Part of a golf course
13 Tell ___ (don't tell the truth): 2 words
14 Astonishment
15 Ending for "respect"
16 Place, like on the Internet
17 Amount at an auction
18 Ice cream flavor: 2 words
21 Shade of brown
22 It lives in a hive
23 Room in a prison
24 Ending for "count" or "baron"
25 "Mighty ___ Young" (movie about a gorilla)
27 Separate with a sieve
30 2000 pounds
31 Music recordings, for short
34 Ice cream flavor: 2 words
38 X-___ vision (one of Superman's powers)

39 Direction on a compass
40 Green citrus fruit
41 Munched on
42 Not early
43 Last word of a prayer
44 What the P stands for in "MPH"
45 Moved quickly
46 Annoying person

DOWN

1 The long, thin part of an arrow
2 Snake that has a hood
3 Woody ___ (famous movie director)
4 "Where have you ___?"
5 Makes potatoes ready for eating
6 ___ Oyl (Popeye's girlfriend)
7 Bread that has a pocket
8 Looked at
9 Kitchen furniture
10 "___ Always Love You" (Whitney Houston song): 2 words
11 What an Olympic winner gets

19 One of the TV networks

20 Cubes that are in the freezer

24 "And on and on": Abbreviation

25 Wrote down in a hurry

26 Half of two

27 ___ heap (pile of junk)

28 "___ you!" ("You're not my friend anymore!"): 2 words

29 Area near the front door, in some houses

30 Try the food

31 Wind ___ (thing that hangs outside and makes jingly sounds)

32 Ten-cent coins

33 Used cash

35 Nighttime birds with big eyes

36 Jump

37 Applaud

38

ACROSS

1 "Get ___ my back!"
4 Joint near the middle of the body
7 Command a dog learns in obedience school
11 ___ Blanc (person who did the voice of Bugs Bunny)
12 They go on kings or twos in the card game spit
14 State where Cincinnati is
15 "Prince ___" (song in the movie "Aladdin")
16 You go camping in one
17 Person who's not cool
18 Presses on a horn
20 "I'm ___ kidding!"
22 The Mediterranean ___
23 Prefix for "gravity" or "freeze"
24 Big structure in Egypt
26 Five-pointed thing
28 Important test
29 Home music systems
31 Health resorts
34 "___ says so?"
35 It's used to make roads
36 Copy of a magazine

37 ___ and rave (argue loudly)
39 Word that appears on the thing at 6-Down
41 Kind of poem (homophone for "owed")
42 Like the numbers 2, 4, and 6
43 Tools for gardeners
44 Tiny nibble
45 What a bird builds
46 Place for a pig
47 "Help us!"

DOWN

1 Big city in Nebraska
2 Criminal
3 Cartoon set in caveman times, with "The"
4 Head coverings
5 Put frosting on a cake
6 Small coin
7 Father's boy
8 Cartoon set in Springfield: 2 words
9 Showed on television, for example

10 Wise creature in the "Star Wars" films

13 Shopping places

19 "Go fly a ___!"

21 What the Internal Revenue Service collects

24 "Practice what you ___!"

25 Boston's state: Abbreviation

27 Paintings and so on

29 Get rid of a beard

30 Cookies with white middles

32 Word that can go before "visual"

33 Oozes

34 Small brown bird

36 "The ___-Bitsy Spider"

38 Stuff that can cause an explosion: Abbreviation

40 A fisherman might throw it into the water

39

ACROSS

1 What keys fit into
6 "___ my pleasure"
9 Get at a store
12 Musical that includes the song "Tomorrow"
13 "How ___ you?"
14 Sly ___ fox: 2 words
15 Kriss Kringle's other name
16 Mother
17 Uncle ___ (symbol of America)
18 Word that might end a list: Abbreviation
20 Little ___ Muffet
22 Work in the movies
25 Big chunk of something
27 "I made a mistake!"
30 ___ of (in a way)
32 A while ___ (in the past)
33 Someone who isn't interesting
34 What the "big hand" points to
35 Some people pay it every month
37 "Do ___ Pass Go …" (phrase in the game Monopoly)
38 It can go before "skirt" or "van"

40 You might get it pierced
42 ___ code (number at the end of an address)
44 Now ___ then
46 The end of one of Aesop's Fables
50 Card with just one symbol on it
51 Split ___ soup
52 Run away to get married
53 "___ out of here!"
54 Messy place
55 Did some stitching

DOWN

1 ___ Vegas
2 "I'm ___ roll!" ("Nothing is going wrong!"): 2 words
3 TV channel that shows mostly news
4 Toy that has a long tail
5 Chairs
6 "Do you know who ___?": 2 words
7 Orchestra instrument
8 Prefix for "finals" or "annual"

9 Orchestra instrument
10 Country formed in 1776: Abbreviation
11 Vegetable also called a sweet potato
19 Orchestra instrument
21 Weep loudly
22 What's left after something is burned
23 Sound a pigeon makes
24 Orchestra instrument
26 Number of years you've been around

28 ___ wrestling (Hulk Hogan's sport)
29 All ___ (ready to go)
31 Beginning for "cycle"
36 Makes less wild
39 Takes a short sleep
41 Part in a play
42 Zig and ___
43 Skating surface
45 24 hours
47 Pull on the oars
48 Monkey's big relative
49 Didn't follow

ACROSS

1 Small restaurant
5 What "expectorate" is a fancy word for
9 Received
12 "I cannot tell ___": 2 words
13 Very, very small
14 ___ de Janeiro, Brazil
15 Color of a carnation
16 Bring in the crops
17 Every last one
18 Enjoy a winter sport
19 ___-tac-toe
20 Possessed
22 Breaks free
25 Opposite of "subtract"
26 Wish
27 Surf and ___ (steak and seafood dinner)
29 ___ Baba
30 Take ___ measures (do something desperate)
33 Grin
35 "___ you kidding?"
36 A bolt fits into it
38 Wrestling hold
39 Desire
41 Truth or ___
42 Grow older
43 Border
44 Something ___ (not this)
45 Negative answers
46 Item planted in a garden
47 "Children should be ___ and not heard"

DOWN

1 Baseball players wear them
2 Similar
3 Ends of races: 2 words
4 What some people say when they see a mouse
5 Having a zebra design
6 Part of a jigsaw puzzle
7 One ___ million: 2 words
8 "Teh" instead of "the," for example
9 Big ending: 2 words
10 Applied grease to

11 Was a tattletale
19 Kind of dancing
21 What a frog supposedly can give you
23 Metal spring
24 Began
28 "___ only as directed"
29 Friend, in Spanish
31 Place for target practice

32 Say swear words
33 Have a short attention ___
34 They baa
37 Someone who's not 20 yet
40 Suffix for "lemon" or "Gator"
41 ___ Moines

ANSWERS

Puzzle 1

```
D A D A   T O O   C O A T
A L O T   R I B   A L S O
M I C H A E L J O R D A N
      E Y E   E A T
W A Y N E   A C T   H A Y
A G E S   L I T   C A S E
R O T   N O R   O A S I S
      P O T   S U M
S C O T T I E P I P P E N
H A D A   O W E   U R G E
E N D S   N E D   S O O T
```

Puzzle 2

```
  P O P   P E A   T E A
  P A N E   I L L   H R S
V I C E P R E S I D E N T
A P E S   A C E   A S I A
T E D   T I E   S T E E R
      S O N   P I E
B U T T E   G O T   R A W
I S E E   W A R   P O L E
T H E W H I T E H O U S E
T E N   A R E   I N T O
Y R S   Y E S   D Y E
```

Puzzle 3

```
L E T S   C T S   A M E N
A L O T   R I O   T A X I
D E N Y   I N N   A R A T
S C I   E M A I L   I C E
  T B O N E   C A R A T
  R U T   B A H
  B A R E R   F E N C E
S O X   R E P E L   A R E
U N T O   C O W   O R A L
I G O R   A P E   D E S K
T O N E   P E R   D Y E S
```

Puzzle 4

```
P I L L   S O F A   F O R
O D I E   U N I T   R Y E
D O D G E B A L L   E L M
    S A M   L A K E
W A S   T I C   S I D E S
A T O P   T A P   D O V E
R A D I O   B A D   M E T
    A N T S   S O B
H I P   H O P S C O T C H
U N O   E R I E   O H N O
G A P   R E E D   K E N T
```

Puzzle 5

```
H E S   I L L   R U S H
O A T   S E E   A S I A
T R A N S F O R M E R S
    P O U T   U P S
F A L S E   H I S   M A Y
A B E E   T I N   L A N E
R E D   S A D   B A N D S
    R E X   A R M S
B E A N I E B A B I E S
E G G S   A L I   O W E
D O S E   T E N   N E T
```

Puzzle 6

```
J A Y S   P A L   E G G S
O R E O   I C E   A R I A
B E L L   N E T   R A N G
    L A S T   T E N N
S H O R T   H E R   D O G
H O W   O P E R A   C U E
Y E S   V A N   S M A R T
    T H E N   R E I N
S H O O   A P E   T Y P E
H A N G   M A N   T O E S
E Y E S   A N T   S N A P
```

7

A	B	E	L		O	N	A		S	H	E
M	A	G	I	C		R	A	T		T	O	Y
A	N	G	E	L		A	G	O		E	W	E
		S	I	G	N		P	A	R		
A	B	C		M	E	G		L	E	T	S
R	O	O	T	B	E	E	R	F	L	O	A	T
M	O	V	E		J	O	E		S	P	Y
	E	N	D		U	T	A	H		
B	A	R		A	L	I		S	A	L	A	D
O	R	E		D	E	C		T	R	A	C	E
B	E	D		S	E	E		D	Y	E	S

8

R	U	M		P	O	E	T		B	Y	T	E
I	N	A		I	D	E	A		R	A	I	L
M	O	N	O	P	O	L	Y		A	H	E	M
		H	E	R		L	I	N	T		
I	N	T	O		P	O	T		Z	A	P
T	O	W		S	T	A	R	S		E	W	E
A	S	I		K	I	D		J	E	E	P
	S	H	I	N		G	O	O		
P	E	T	E		S	C	R	A	B	B	L	E
E	V	E	R		E	D	I	T		B	O	Y
W	E	R	E		L	E	N	S		S	U	E

9

A	N	T		F	A	T		B	A	G
D	R	A	W		T	A	M	E		A	G	O
R	E	M	O	T	E	C	O	N	T	R	O	L
O	N	E		W	E	T	S		H	O	O	D
P	T	S		I	N	S		S	E	N	D
		I	C	Y		W	H	Y		
C	U	T	E		P	E	A		C	O	W
O	H	N	O		S	L	A	P		A	P	E
M	I	C	R	O	W	A	V	E	O	V	E	N
I	L	L		C	A	N	E		R	E	N	T
T	E	E		T	N	T		E	S	S

10

H	A	S		M	T	S		G	O	A	T
A	L	E		P	R	O	P		A	M	M	O
W	O	W		H	A	L	O		B	A	B	Y
K	N	E	W		M	E	G	A		H	E	S
	G	R	A	S	P		O	S	C	A	R
		D	U	O		S	I	R		
	S	T	E	E	L		T	A	I	L	S
W	H	O		Z	I	T	I		B	A	T	S
R	A	T	S		N	I	C	E		N	O	T
A	R	E	A		E	L	K	S		E	V	E
P	E	S	T		T	S	P		S	E	W

11

L	O	B	E		L	A	C	E		F	A	N
I	L	A	Y		A	M	A	N		R	I	O
M	I	K	E		V	E	S	T		E	S	S
E	V	E		S	A	S	H		O	N	L	Y
	E	D	I	T		S	E	A	N	C	E
		P	O	E	M		W	I	T	H	
	T	O	U	P	E	E		L	O	F	T
W	I	T	S		N	A	P	S		R	E	N
I	M	A		C	A	S	E		F	I	N	E
M	E	T		A	C	E	S		L	E	S	S
P	R	O		B	E	L	T		U	S	E	S

12

I	L	L		O	F	F		B	A	R	B	S
T	E	A		T	U	B		A	L	O	O	K
S	T	P	A	T	R	I	C	K	S	D	A	Y
		H	E	S		L	E	O		
F	A	V	O	R		J	A	R		N	E	T
A	W	A	Y		N	A	P		L	O	V	E
D	E	N		S	E	W		S	I	R	E	N
		W	A	R		R	A	P		
A	P	R	I	L	F	O	O	L	S	D	A	Y
R	A	I	S	E		F	A	T		A	L	E
T	Y	P	E	S		A	D	S		M	A	T

88

13

```
D A D S   C O B S   E L F
A L I E   O V A L   P I E
R I S E   D E N Y   C A R
K E N   S E N D   C O R N
  N E S T S   S H O T S
    Y O U     A R C
  S W U N G   C I D E R
S T O P   R E A L   N E T
O A R   R A G S   I T S A
I L L   E D G E   S E E P
L E D   M E S S   A R T S
```

14

```
H A S   A G E S   W A I T
E N T   S O L O   A N D A
A G O   H A M B U R G E R
R E N O   L E S S   E A T
  R E P A I R   H I L L
    I N E   M E T
  T R E K   S I R E N S
S H E   L A W N   M A T S
P E P P E R O N I   M O E
A R E A   T R O T   E V E
R E L Y   S E W S   D E N
```

15

```
P E T   S O S   R A B B I
O W E   E A T   A L L E N
P E A N U T S   L I O N S
      E S S   O P E N
W A D E S   B A H   D A Y
A C I D   P E R   W I N E
G E L   B A G   W E E D S
    B I L L   P A N
G E E S E   F O X T R O T
O G R E S   A G E   A R E
T O T E S   R O D   P E N
```

16

```
L A W   S C A N   B A I L
A G O   T A C O   E L M O
S E R P E N T S   A L P S
  L A P       C D S
L A D Y   B O A R   T I P
I T S   F U N N Y   A C E
T E E   A M E N   C R E W
  R E X     L O G
R A I N   S I D E W A Y S
U S E D   O V E N   M E A
B A S S   B E N D   E N D
```

17

```
J A B S   R A P   M A S T
I S E E   E S T   U T A H
F A N T A S I A   L A T E
    A M I   S P A
T I S   U S E   O N I O N
I N K   S T A R E   T W O
M A Y B E   R O T   S E W
    A D S   A I M
W A R M   H E R C U L E S
A R A B   I V E   L A S T
S E M I   N E D   E Y E S
```

18

```
  S C A R   H I P   W E B
S H A P E   O R E   A L A
L I N E N   M O N S T E R
A N T S   K E N   P E C K
P E A   A I R   P A R T
  L A S T   F A R M
  R O C K   T A N   E L F
T O U R   P I N   F L E E
E M P E R O R   A L O N E
L E E   A G E   M E N D S
L O S   N O D   P A S S
```

19

T	O	S	S		A	T	M		F	L	U
I	N	C	A		M	E	A		T	R	I	P
S	E	I	N	F	E	L	D		O	I	L	S
			T	A	N		R	I	P	E	
S	O	F	A	R		T	I	N		N	F	L
E	A	R		M	A	I	D	S		D	I	E
E	R	A		E	S	P		I	T	S	N	O
	S	O	R	T		A	D	E		
R	A	I	D		R	O	S	E	A	N	N	E
I	C	E	D		O	A	K		R	O	B	S
P	E	R		S	T	S		S	W	A	T

20

T	I	E	S			C	R	I	B
S	T	R	E	A	K		K	A	R	A	T	E
P	A	N	A	M	A		O	B	E	Y	E	D
		T	I	N		A	C	E	
L	A	B	S		G	A	L		P	O	P	E
A	R	E		A	L	A		W	I	N
S	T	E	W		R	I	B		S	L	E	D
		A	G	O		E	A	T	
S	T	E	R	E	O		A	P	A	C	H	E
H	O	L	M	E	S		R	E	L	I	E	S
Y	A	M	S				L	A	M	P

21

M	A	P		B	A	A	S		D	A	D	S
A	L	A		A	R	C	H		O	P	E	N
N	O	R		D	I	N	E		C	O	L	A
O	N	E	S		D	E	E	R		S	I	P
	G	N	O	M	E		P	O	S	T	S
		T	R	Y		S	I	R	
	R	H	E	T	T		V	E	N	O	M
S	H	E		H	O	M	E		S	P	O	T
P	I	S	A		W	I	R	E		H	O	E
A	N	E	W		E	L	S	E		E	S	S
N	O	S	E		R	E	E	L		S	E	T

22

B	A	L	D		B	A	D		S	E	E	D
I	T	O	R		O	L	E		P	A	N	E
B	A	S	E	B	A	L	L	C	A	R	D	S
			W	A	R		L	A	D	
H	A	S		A	D	S		T	E	L	L	S
A	T	O	P		S	A	D		S	A	I	L
T	E	X	A	S		W	E	D		S	P	Y
		S	U	M		A	I	R	
F	O	O	T	B	A	L	L	G	A	M	E	S
E	R	I	E		T	I	E		C	A	G	E
W	E	L	L		H	E	R		E	D	G	E

23

S	A	P	S		F	E	W		C	A	T
C	L	U	E		S	O	L	E		A	L	E
A	B	L	E		O	U	S	T		T	I	E
B	U	S		H	U	L	A		B	E	E	S
	M	E	R	I	T		L	E	A	R	N
		A	S	H		V	A	N	
	B	R	I	S	K		A	R	G	U	E
B	R	A	N		O	D	D	S		N	A	G
O	A	K		O	R	E	O		K	I	T	E
I	V	E		W	E	A	R		I	T	E	M
L	E	D		L	A	D		D	E	N	S

24

B	A	B	E		W	A	V	Y		G	E	M
A	R	A	T		E	X	A	M		E	A	R
D	E	B	T		T	E	N	C	E	N	T	S
	Y	E	S			A	G	E	
R	O	B		I	R	O	N		G	R	I	P
I	D	O		S	A	F	E	S		A	S	A
O	D	O	R		G	A	T	E		T	A	N
	M	A	D		A	S	I	
I	C	E	W	A	T	E	R		H	O	R	N
N	O	R		M	A	Y	I		O	N	T	O
A	D	S		S	P	E	D		O	X	E	N

25

M	O	B		T	E	A		L	I	F	T	S
A	P	U		O	D	D		A	D	O	R	E
M	E	R	M	A	I	D		S	I	R	E	N
A	N	N	E		T	E	N		D	E	A	D
	S	T	A	R		D	I	P		S	T	S
		S	T	A	Y		P	O	S	T		
A	S	I		G	E	M		D	I	G	S	
C	H	E	R		T	I	P		G	R	E	W
H	O	N	E	Y		N	O	W	H	E	R	E
E	R	N	I	E		T	O	E		E	V	E
D	E	A	N	S		S	H	E		N	E	D

26

M	A	R	S		A	T	A		C	H	A	T
O	H	I	O		R	E	N		L	I	S	A
P	A	D	S		C	A	T	W	O	M	A	N
	D	O	I	T		S	E	W				
P	A	L		N	I	P		I	N	P	U	T
O	L	E		S	C	O	U	R		E	S	E
P	A	R	K	A		E	N	D		N	A	N
		A	N	D		L	O	N	G			
M	R	F	R	E	E	Z	E		A	U	N	T
R	O	L	E		N	O	S		B	I	B	S
S	W	A	N		S	O	S		S	N	A	P

27

L	I	S	T		A	P	E	S		B	A	T
A	S	I	A		D	A	V	E		A	R	E
N	A	N	C	Y	D	R	E	W		L	E	E
D	I	G		A	S	I	N		P	L	A	N
	D	E	E	R		S	T	R	E	S	S	
			E	N	D		S	A	P			
	K	A	N	S	A	S		N	E	A	R	
P	O	L	Y		M	O	O	D		L	O	U
O	R	E		H	A	R	D	Y	B	O	Y	S
P	E	R		A	G	E	D		O	N	C	E
E	A	T		M	E	S	S		B	E	E	S

28

C	A	P	S			A	C	T		J	O	B
A	G	A	I	N		B	O	W		O	N	A
R	O	L	L	E	R	C	O	A	S	T	E	R
			L	E	A		L	I	E			
M	D	S		D	I	P		N	E	W	E	R
P	O	O	F		N	O	T		D	E	W	Y
H	E	L	L	O		T	O	M		B	E	E
			U	P	S		W	A	S			
A	M	U	S	E	M	E	N	T	P	A	R	K
D	O	S		R	O	Y		H	A	S	T	E
O	W	E		A	G	E			T	H	E	Y

29

D	I	G		A	B	C			B	U	L	B
I	N	A		L	A	L	A		I	D	E	A
M	A	U	R	I	C	E	S	E	N	D	A	K
S	I	Z	E		H	A	T	E		E	S	E
	R	E	A	D		T	A	R		R	E	D
			L	E	T		R	I	P			
M	A	P		L	O	A		E	A	T	S	
A	L	A		T	U	B	A		P	I	E	D
R	I	C	H	A	R	D	S	C	A	R	R	Y
S	K	E	E		S	U	I	T		E	V	E
H	E	R	S			L	A	S		D	E	S

30

A	B	C		W	E	B			S	W	A	Y
C	A	R		A	M	I		S	T	O	R	E
E	Y	E		R	U	G		H	U	N	T	S
		D	A	M		A	R	A	B			
S	H	I	P			S	U	M		S	N	O
C	U	T	E	A	S	A	B	U	T	T	O	N
I	N	S		B	A	H			H	A	T	E
			T	O	T	O		B	E	T		
T	O	Y	O	U		U	S	E		I	T	S
A	R	E	N	T		S	E	E		O	W	E
N	E	T	S			E	A	T		N	O	W

31

```
PAT   OAR   ART
ALI   RIO   LIRA
ROLLERBLADING
THEO  SEE   SODA
SASSY SAD   SAG
   SAN   FOG
DOS   MUD   CLAMP
EATS  MOM   AREA
SKATEBOARDING
 SLAW  RYE   SUE
 EYE   SOX   ESS
```

32

```
RIP   PEGS  RACE
ONE   OXEN  ILAY
TAN   LIMOUSINE
   POET   USE
STARS  PTA   FED
HOLE   HIS   SOAR
YES    FOG   PARTS
   AIR   NAME
SPORTSCAR   VAN
HALT   EAST  EGO
ENDS   STAY  RED
```

33

```
SAGS   ESP    ASA
EXIT   RAIL   GAG
WERE   ANTELOPE
   APES   TOE
OFF    TEN    EGGS
ALF    CRUST  OAK
RYES    TEA   RBI
   IAM   ANDI
ELEPHANT   ALSO
NEW    SMEE   SLAW
DIE    ADD    HATE
```

34

```
TACKS  THE   JOY
AWAIT  OIL   ALE
ZESTY  ALMONDS
   HELP   LED
ABE   EAR   ROPES
COWS  TOP   RENO
EASEL TEA   ADS
   WAS   PLAN
WALNUTS   ERUPT
EYE   RUT   RETIE
BEG   ANY   TASTE
```

35

```
TIC   ISIT  GRAM
IDO   JUDO  OHNO
PEN   KNIT  TOGO
SANE  SOSO  DEN
 SECRET  DEER
  CHAT  NOWI
 STOP  CARESS
AMI   SWAT  SLOB
RICH  ABIT  ALA
CLUE  LIVE  NAB
SETS  KNEE  DRY
```

36

```
MET   ALA   SPOON
OWE   NAB   PIANO
PER   NBC   RERAN
   ROAR   MAD
RAIL  AWAY   SCI
USED  DEL   SPAT
BAR   SODA  EARS
   WAR   MEAN
CAMEL  BUY   IAM
ALONE  ATE   EGO
PLOTS  YES   LOW
```

37

```
S C A B   M O P S   T I M
H O L E   A L I E   A W E
A B L E   S I T E   B I D
F R E N C H V A N I L L A
T A N   B E E   C E L L
      E S S   J O E
S I F T   T O N   C D S
C H O C O L A T E C H I P
R A Y   W E S T   L I M E
A T E   L A T E   A M E N
P E R   S P E D   P E S T
```

38

```
O F F   H I P     S T A Y
M E L   A C E S   O H I O
A L I   T E N T   N E R D
H O N K S   N O T   S E A
A N T I   P Y R A M I D
  S T A R   E X A M
  S T E R E O S   S P A S
W H O   T A R   I S S U E
R A N T   C E N T   O D E
E V E N   H O E S   N I P
N E S T     S T Y   S O S
```

39

```
L O C K S   I T S   B U Y
A N N I E   A R E   A S A
S A N T A   M O M   S A M
      E T C   M I S S
A C T   S L A B   O O P S
S O R T   A G O   B O R E
H O U R   R E N T   N O T
    M I N I   E A R
Z I P   A N D   M O R A L
A C E   P E A   E L O P E
G E T   S T Y   S E W E D
```

40

```
C A F E   S P I T   G O T
A L I E   T I N Y   R I O
P I N K   R E A P   A L L
S K I   T I C   O W N E D
  E S C A P E S   A D D
  H O P E   T U R F
  A L I   D R A S T I C
S M I L E   A R E   N U T
P I N   W A N T   D A R E
A G E   E D G E   E L S E
N O S   S E E D   S E E N
```

ABOUT THE AUTHOR

Trip Payne is a professional puzzlemaker living in Atlanta. He currently makes the crossword for the school newsletter *Scholastic News*, and has also made kids' puzzles for the magazines *Games Junior* and *Zigzag*.

His previous Sterling books include *365 Celebrity Crypto-Quotes*, *The Little Giant Encyclopedia of Word Puzzles* (coauthor), and *Mighty Mini Crosswords*. His puzzles can be seen in such places as *The New Yorker*, *The New York Times*, and *TV Guide*.

WHAT IS AMERICAN MENSA?

American Mensa
The High IQ Society
One out of 50 people qualifies
for American Mensa ...
Are YOU the One?

American Mensa, Ltd. is an organization for individuals who have one common trait: a score in the top two percent of the population on a standardized intelligence test. Over five million Americans are eligible for membership ... you may be one of them.

• Looking for intellectual stimulation?
You'll find a good "mental workout" in the *Mensa Bulletin*, our national magazine. Voice your opinion in the newsletter published by your local group. And attend activities and gatherings with fascinating programs and engaging conversation.

• Looking for social interaction?
There's something happening on the Mensa calendar almost daily. These range from lectures to game nights to parties. Each year, there are over 40 regional gatherings and the Annual Gathering, where you can meet people, exchange ideas, and make interesting new friends.

• Looking for others who share your special interest?

Whether your interest might be in computer gaming, Monty Python, or scuba, there's probably a Mensa Special Interest Group (SIG) for you. There are over 150 SIGs, which are started and maintained by members.

So contact us today to receive a free brochure and application.

American Mensa, Ltd.
1229 Corporate Drive West
Arlington, TX 76006
(800) 66-MENSA
AmericanMensa@compuserve.com
http://www.us.mensa.org

If you don't live in the U.S. and would like to get in touch with your national Mensa, contact:

Mensa International
15 The Ivories
6-8 Northampton Street, Islington
London N1 2HY England